A Moment in My Time

By: Michael A Hipp

15 April 2019

I've probably played through this idea a million times in my head. The thought of a book revolving completely around exactly that, my thoughts. Capturing the chaos and the intricacies that, well let's be honest, would probably bore the shit out of you. But here we are, breaking the laws of good sentence structure and talking about just what I'm thinking. So, welcome to boredom, hope it suits you as well as it interests me.

The thought of putting together a novel had always been something of a personal vendetta to me. Not necessarily that I had something to avenge my family for but more so just for the ones inside my head. A little thing to prove to myself because I seem to do a lot of talking. In fact, I have the workings of four chapters full of fictional drunken interestingness that seem to grab a few chuckles and, as I'm told, paint a great picture. Maybe I'll finish said personal mission, maybe I won't but at least it'll be fun the whole way through. Oh, the drunken times I've had, the paper and me. Though I must admit, this whole typed up mess just doesn't have the same sense of feeling to me as scribbled down emotions across a blank slate of openness. Man, I wonder if I talk this way daily between the curse worlds and liquor slurs as well. At least I find it comical. Can't even begin to tell you where this idea originated but here it is, in all its glory. No way it there will be a page a day or some kind of buffoonery in that nature. Let's be realistic for a moment, the only time we should really write down what we're thinking, what we're feeling, is when the moment hits us. Funny how that moment hits me a lot over these years of self-study and bedside drinks. So, saddle up, take a drink, and ready yourself for a little journey to the brain that created the poetry I'm assuming you liked, otherwise you wouldn't be reading this now; this here is the first bit of A Moment in My Time. Let's hope it's a good one.

- M.H.

16 April 2019

Days sometimes feel like a movie, but no one ever tells you what genre it's supposed to be. Maybe that's the biggest secret in life. To determine what movie, it is that we live in. I remember the first time I watched "Stranger Than Fiction" and I always wondered who my author was. Was I the main character waiting to find my impending tragedy or some wannabe sophisticate hoping to change the world whether through tragedy or triumph? See, that's the thing about days; I try to break daily that fourth wall of bullshit we like to compare our lives in and hope that it sets some kind of, like I said, wannabe example for someone who feels like an extra in someone else's story.

In a time where we are so obsessed about colors I still find my affiliations far greyer than concrete. Maybe it's a permanent placement of what I am and where I will fail to go or an open canvas that finds others also lost, feeling stuck, in the same place. I'm interested in the things that make us different shades of blue and purple, but I love in the way that grey fits every good and bad situation. So, excuses are fun in a moment's notice, but never tell the truth of the matter; and I guess the matter is simply that we've stopped being truthful. We've grown so accustomed to this age of online short stories and rumors that we've tried to make them idols. I'm no saint of chivalry and far from the proper gentleman, but I would like to think that I've learned and loved in ways that have graced me in some abstract form of wisdom. But then again, aren't I just that borderline alcoholic that feels the same way as you do? Funny the times we romanticized the idea of being the movie everyone else wanted to see; let's get back to being the cinematic creation everyone's to scarred but needs to breathe.

- M.H.

17 April 2019

You know, I should really be doing the homework I've been procrastinating instead of writing this ramble of left brained shit, but here we are. I thought of something earlier that, typically, I would roll into some form of a poem. At least that's how I felt when I read it back over, noticing it feels an awful lot like old poems I churned up in the past.

The only difference between thoughts and smoke is that one gets to burn and drift away; the other just burns and sits with you on the nights you wish you had everything to say.

I can't even begin to fathom the amount of times I've written about the symbolism of smoking cigarettes. There's just something lively about killing a small piece of yourself five to ten minutes at a time. For those anti-smokers that are already rolling your eyes preparing the most hair on the back of the neck trembling shriek of, "You should really quit", sorry buckaroo, not on my current interest plate. It's okay to care about my health, truly, all of us smokers appreciate it, but if we wanted to quit then we would do it on our own not because someone told us to. I mean, did you really think that you convince someone that's already accepted the fact that the thing they find momentary solace in kills them little by little to stop? Once again there dude braj, sorry not going to happen. There's just something about it that brings this humbling sense of sobriety to everything around you, allowing you five to ten minutes where we get to simply sit and enjoy the things around us and if we have to pay with minutes of our life just to appreciate the life that we have, well fuck bud, that's more than worth it to me.

When it comes down to the brass tacks of it all, the thing about smoking, for me, is that it's time I have to myself where I can take any thought that has been burning a hole in my head and my heart for that day and simply set it free. I know this originally started with a sense of being worn down by thoughts but it also reminded me about how great those moments to myself can be. So, invite the reaper the next time you're out for smoke, ask him what he thinks about the whole thing. By the way, he's the biggest addict of us all because he gets to spend every second we take a

drag taking another piece of us and sometimes, that's really all we

need.

- M.H.

18 April 2019

As I said in the first page, this pile of paper with a bunch of off the rocker thoughts has been something that I've been mulling over for quite some time now. So, like any other less than normal person with an estranged affinity for an idea they came up with, it had to start somewhere. Looking back, I can think of many times that I sat down and wrote out some passage or even poorly written short story dating back to high school when I first started finding an addiction for the way words work in the ways of thought, feeling, and sound. However, for some reason I can't even think about what all of those were about. I'm sure in my prepubescent state it came off as some master piece of thoughts and feelings that I would think to one day wow some future love of my life. Older, not necessarily more mature, me has an inkling that it's going to come off quite cringe worthy, but maybe we'll venture down that path together while I consider putting my past writing ventures into this here stack of "entertainment".

There is one particular page I wrote that I have been thinking about a lot lately. Now, I haven't read this thing over since the day it was written and there's even a possibility that I wrote it in a completely different time than my slowly old deteriorating memory would like to tell me. The important thing, is that I remember where I got the idea from and I'm going to try and remember what I was trying to interpret. This was back when I was withering away for a few years in Oklahoma and if it is in the time I'm remembering, it was right around the time I met someone that would go on to be Miss ex-fiancé whom I do not wish to speak to ever again (Not that I don't care for her, just that there's simply no need for that negativity in my life anymore). I remember laying in my bed one night, probably binging the fuck out of some TV show about World War II. When, I noticed this little spot on the TV that had just gone black. Of course, it took my slow and tired ass until the damned thing moved to realize that it was a fly. For the life of me I don't know why this idea came to my head, but it did. I thought about what it would be like to be a fly on a TV screen. To be in the way of what the human was watching on the ceremonial box of lights and amazement, perhaps just trying to enjoy it myself. It got me thinking about my life and my current situation at the time and how I could be the fly on the TV to the woman I had currently taken quite the affection for. It went on for an entire notebook page, maybe a page and a half, and by then I believe I had begun dating and signing all of the things I was writing. I guess I'll just have to dig through my mountain of notebooks and find that old thought provoking beauty to throw in here. It's weird though, I've written poems so emotionally driven that a piece of me could literally be found in the punctuation marks, but honestly, not sure that I would recognize it at first glance. There are even songs I wrote when I first started writing music equally as from the heart that I can't remember how to play, but this one passage. This one moment in my time has still stuck with me to this day. Ramblings of a drunken fool or not, I think that shits pretty fucking cool. (Que strange laughter).

- M.H.

19 April 2019

I love words, but I'm horrible at reading. What I mean by that, before you pin me down as some illiterate piece of shit that literally lived in a Thesaurus just to write any of this, is that I can't even remember the last time I actually finished a book. I have this thing for picking up a book, reading anywhere from a quarter to half of it, and then becoming so beyond inspired with ideas that I put it down and start writing myself. One time, a quote from Benjamin Franklin inspired a song of mine that truly made me feel like I was making progress in my musical aspirations. I think I read maybe two or three chapters and never picked up that book again. Though, the worst part of it all was that it wasn't even a book by Ben Franklin, he was simply quoted in it. Great read so far, definitely plan to finish it one day.

I have what they call a restless mind which makes it impossible to spend time without multitasking and an absolute chore to attempt the great worldly pass time of sleep. Yet, I wonder why I have such a hard time with reading. When I was a child I used to get in trouble for the hours I would stay up late to read books about wizards, knights, and dragons. In fact, one time I even read a book by the light of a tiny alarm clock because I knew I was up far later than I was supposed to be and the book was too perfect. The last series I remember divulging into was about vampires with a hint of adult styled comedy and gore that started to peak my interest into something a little more mature in the world of written fiction. Little did I know that would lead to me developing a love for writers like Poe, Hemmingway, and Bukowski. Believe it or not, the last book I actually finished the whole way through was a book by Hemmingway and it made me want to buy more and more. So, I did, and there they sit on my bookshelf still waiting for "one day" to happen. Let's just ignore the fact that I'm still only three quarters of the way through a book by Charles Bukowski that honestly makes me want to stuff my face back into those blood-soaked pages hoping to simply absorb some form of resemblance to the style ole man Bukowski could kill it with. Definitely a book I will finish, "one day". I keep saying "one day" because it makes me think a lot about all of the times I said one day about things that I wanted to do, things I wanted to create myself. It took me a long time to finally find an intersection between the phrases one day and today, but I found it. Three mediocre poetry books, a shit ton of music that at least someone likes (Me), and this thing you're hopefully holding in your hands to read. The thing is, before then I had this weird way of not being me but trying to make myself look like the me I always wanted to be. Now, I'm just that guy who turns on music, pours a glass of whiskey, and flies through poetry books by people who inspire me simply because it puts my mind in a place that just can't stop generating what I call creative, but others surely define as self-therapy. "One Day" we just stop being scared to be who we were meant to be and accept the fact that it's never going to be everyone's cup of whiskey, mostly because not everyone likes whiskey; I'm sure you get the meaning. Hopefully, you read this in decent terms, "one day".

- M.H.

22 April 2019

The past few days I have been thinking a lot about what influenced me to become this mess you see before you trying to speak through dried ink and words we all pretended to read in high school. If I'm being completely honest, this is more than likely going to come up more than once because there are so many things that helped me become this interesting little sad fun bag of endless words and drinks. Thing is, all of that thinking, it made me think of one particular thing that I haven't thought about in a long time.

Everyone has to get started somewhere, for me, in retrospect to writing, that started in high school. A little background to that however; I grew up loving old school rock and later that turned my interests to punk rock and later on heavier and heavier. I know this sounds like rambling, but its relevant, so chill the fuck out! In the younger years, I always had an attachment to the lyrics and constantly felt like I was the only one that actual felt them while I watched others sing them with the lack of emotion. Just purely spitting out some horrid word garbage to feel cool, but it meant so much to me. This was all happening in middle school by the way. The good stuff happens in high school, like I said. Freshman year of high school, my rebellious and yet still somehow nerdy ass was in marching band, where I made a mortal enemy. Well, he started out as a someone I hated and actually turned into one of the best friends I had. However, if memory serves me correctly, and the Gatorade he poured in my long curly locks from back then didn't permanently fry my brain, it took until later that year and maybe into sophomore year for that friendship to truly spark. All of which started with an apology for the Gatorade incident and a mutual love for similar music, especially as I had just taken steps into the heavier side of the music world. I won't mention the guy's name, but I hope that if he one day reads this pile of garbage that he can appreciate it. My buddy was a drummer, had been in a couple of bands, by bands I mean the group of our friends getting together and preforming covers at Halloween parties and what not. Either way more experience. Me being the young saxophonist in the school band and slowly, and sure enough horribly, teaching myself guitar was impressed with his experience in the lack thereof in my own. I'm not sure why, but with my minimal talent in the subject, ole boy wanted me to do vocals for a band and originally play guitar, but trust me there was no way I was going to be able to play guitar for the style of band we were trying to make. However, he had me convinced on the bass. Yes, I'm sure you're dying to know, but it was a death metal band and we were going to call ourselves, "The Devils Rejects" after the famed Rob Zombie movie. We had a whole album concept idea worked out incorporating Freddy Kruger and a few other horror greats. It was a fun idea that never took fruition, but was a constant talk between the two of us and later a guitarist that we had met along the way. Oh, by the way, it was a Christian death metal band, so a lot of our music was going to be super bible oriented. Me, growing up the Irish Italian Catholic that is my family, saw no issues with this what so ever, but felt I was looking for something a little more out there and rebellious (remember I was a teenager) … (well, I guess I never really grew out of that now did I?) but it became my first opportunity to try my hand at writing. Since I was doing the vocals, I had to come up with the lyrics. The extent of my writing prowess at the time was that of rhyming couplets I had learned about in some English class and the extensive amount of music that I had grown up around. So, I took a stab at the bitch and tried my best.

I still have the notes my friend left me, basically changing the whole thing that I wrote (yes, I still laugh at how horrible both of us were). My idea was strictly rhyming couplets at the time and because of that the best line of advice was dropped on me in my writing adolescence. "Don't write to rhyme like everyone else, write a story". I'm paraphrasing of course, but it changed the way I looked at my writing. I stopped writing within the confines of the rules and start just adapting this free verse style of lyrical poetry, which honestly was still horrible. But we loved it and our idea (notice how I broke a big grammar rule there in this sentence again, rules are for chumps!).

Thing was, after all of these ideas and almost things that happened, my buddy changed from the emotional, rebellious, metal head we all knew and loved into some preppy boy because he had started dating some girl. Not a huge deal, because I was never one to judge anyone for the clothes they chose to wear but rather for whether or not they were truly a good person or not. He was a good person and we still remained friends. Even sat next to each other in English class.

Not going to lie, this is a hard one to write about. One day we were sitting there in English class and my friend passed me a note. Followed by a few more after I sent back responses. These notes stayed in my wallet for years to come and the only reason they aren't anymore is because they fell out after someone decided to go through said wallet years later. I can't remember the exact words, but it was a way of telling me he was going to kill himself, and I remember seeing the seriousness in his eyes. Trying to find the joke in the matter, waiting for him to crack a smile and show me that he truly didn't mean it, but it never came. So, I walked with him following class, trying to talk him out of it. Trying to plead him to just come to lunch with me like we always had. But he didn't and I watched him walk out the door. To this day, this was one of the scariest days of my life. I didn't know what to do, but I ran my ass to the lunch room and found another friend of ours explaining the situation. Next thing I know I'm speaking with principles and telling them that my best friend had gone off to kill himself by hanging himself with his own belt. Sorry, if this isn't as creative as everything else in here, this is the first time I've talked about this in a long time.

Long story short, they found him and he was safe. The friendship we had kind of just disintegrated from there, but we would still talk every now and again. For those of you wondering, he ended up happy and has a family now. He's alive and well. The biggest thing I never got to thank him for though, since we don't talk anymore, is the influence he had on my writing. He shaped a lot of the things I was into and the things I wrote about. I took his advice and brought back the rhyming couplets, but with my own feel to it. Everything I wrote from there on out was a story in its own. And I never followed the rules with it. The greatest writers learn all of the rules so they know how to break them properly. I personally learned them and said fuck it all together because it meant more to me and to those that read it. Shitty situation, but here I am, still writing multiple years later.

- M.H.

23 April 2019

So, I found the one about being a fly on the TV screen, but I was so incredibly wrong as to the timeframe. In fact, I didn't even date the page at all and I'm slightly upset about it, but I did promise I would share it, so here it is. Also, I found a bunch of other "journal entries" that I found interesting and may drop the old days of words past on this growing project we have here. Without any further fucking ado:

"You know, I've always wondered what it'd be like to be that bug on the TV screen. Does he only see the small pixilation in front of him or the masterful big picture that we dull our minds with? Hell, does he live and feel like we do? From a human stand point, I personally think that none of us have even factored that in. In fact, as far as I'm concerned, from that previous spoken position, the bug just merely existed. Slowly moving from one side of the screen to the other as we finish our episode, just waiting for the moment that you finally get your lazy ass off the couch and swat it away. But does this single, tiny, what was thought insignificant life form not even ponder the slightest possibility of harm coming its way? Fuck, as I write this I can virtually see my original thesis changing. To begin with I was going to make some point about perceiving the big picture as opposed to being what most would call stubborn, but I'm starting to see as passion. Because, as many times as you put a hand in front of the bug and obstruct its path, it still keeps moving forward. Whether that be through the new mountainous road ahead or even the easy road around it, it still soldiers on. So, to blatantly re-state and full circle this random metaphor I began with, it seems I've found my answer in writing. The bug sees the big picture, but he follows the small pixilation's to create his own masterful scene."

As we can see, I was most definitely a few sheets to the wind and attempting to sound intelligent while also finding something I found beautiful between the lines. Strange the words of the drunken lost looking for peace in the little things.

- M.H.

24 April 2019

Honestly, didn't think that I would even write today.
Actually, I've been thinking that every day so far, but somehow
something just pops in my head. I started keeping a list of certain
topics I would talk about in this book; which is completely against
who I am in the realms of writing and music. In a world so strict on
structure, I find that the most beautiful and heart-felt things come
in the moment and are never forced or practiced. In fact, the only
form of practice or writing exercise I have done myself, and later
on advised to others in search of advice, was to train your brain to
shutoff when writing. Make everything come completely from the
heart. I was lucky enough to have someone that taught me back in
my beginning stages of writing and let me tell you, I was not great
at it at first. For some reason, I felt the importance at first was to be
overly descriptive of layouts and scenes. It was as if I wanted to
paint a picture so vivid in words that Michelangelo would shed a
tear at the image his mind made from reading it. Now, the kicker to
that is that as my writing habits matured my adolescent use of too

much imagery helped me to pave together metaphors that I would never expected to happen. In my learning experiences, I would actually spend a class period prior to my creative writing class searching for a picture to write about in the first fifteen minutes we spent strictly writing. No conversation, no interaction, and surely no stopping. Just fifteen pure minutes of genuine silence surrounded by the whispers of emotions that we were afraid to let out. I loved that class. To this day, I still have the notebook I used for it and that was one of the first times I started getting more confident about my writing. This is something that I will probably blab on about again later because I found a great little piece I wrote about the teacher I had during this class that turned my whole idea of writing around.

Remember how I said I didn't even plan on writing today? This whole page is literally a Jackson Pollock of what happens when I start writing. Originally, I had a completely different idea that compelled me to scour the house for the last bit of whiskey around and set up behind this here damned keyboard. Though, I like where it went in the end. I guess that's the beauty in all of this,

letting things pour out when it's least expected, feeling completely

vulnerable in inanimate objects, and finding not only yourself but

your heart in a world that constantly wants you to suppress it.

- M.H.

25 April 2019

So, to back track a bit and talk about the idea my hands decided to not type about yesterday. Music. Sweet, beautiful, deep, painful, and overall fulfilling, music. I'm sure this will be brought up just as much as my affinity for the written word throughout this lame old journey together. The main thing that has just been absolutely rattling around in my head and honestly, my heart the past few days, has been how just one song can take you back to a completely different time, a completely different world. Days of life's past. Maybe that's why I find myself keener to that of the sadder side of the music world. Sadness brings out the realism in a person. Though we walk about with smiles, we have this certain……. Fuck. I've fried my brain on school work, work, and coping with everyday stress and I'm struggling to put down on page what it is I wanted to say to begin with. I'm laughing as I type these lines because it just sits too perfectly with what I was going to say to begin with.

Music has had this weird possession of me for as long as I can remember. Whether good or bad…. Yeah, I'm just going to stab at this a different time.

- M.H.

5 May 2019

I started going back through my old writing notebooks.
Dumb idea, especially when you're just looking for a piece
specifically to fit this book and then you're bombarded with
thoughts and feelings of every bit of past. Though, while trudging
my way through each blood-stained page, I noticed where I first
started adding my signature at the end of every piece. Not going to
lie, it looked weird as fuck at first and I kept doing it that way for a
while. Que the cringe worthy memes. But, it made me think about
why I started doing it in the first place. I truly don't even know
where I picked it up from. At the time, I was starting to make a
small name for myself in the online writing community, nothing
special and it sure as fuck never became anything more than that,
but I had a fan base and I had people seeking me out for writing
advice. Honestly, I probably noticed that all of the writers I aspired
to be like in this digital world used their fancy typewriters to tap
their own initials or name into a page for eternity. Everything
about that just resonated with my weirdness and wanting to be

proud of what I had done, whether it was shit or not. I was always taught that if you're proud of your work you shouldn't be afraid to put your name on it, and I know that was meant to be metaphorical in order to produce better results in a working environment but I took it seriously. The idea of taking something that was so genuinely yours and to put your own personal stamp on it had just this oddly fulfilling effect on me. So, I changed my lame ass signature and we have what you see at the end of each of my mosh pits worth of thoughts and ideals jotted down and dried with yesterday's cum rag. But, that's my little cum rag, every bit of it, just look at the name inscribed at the bottom.

- M.H.

7 May 2019

It took me nearly an entire work day to figure out what music to listen to while I try to recapture this whole thing I was thinking about the other day. In fact, it was a conversation that I had with a good friend of mine. Making our way across Germany to a city we had bought concert tickets in. Fuck, I wish I could recreate perfectly the conversation, though isn't that what makes real life memories just a little bit better than the stories? Knowing that certain things will never be as great for those who weren't even involved. So, after taking an entire day to decide on the music to write to and a few drinks to attempt and relive that drunken conversation, let's talk about keeping your hands out of your fucking pockets.

Now before we venture further into this, for those of you who are reading this (all three of you) that do not know, I was in the military for a fair portion of my early twenties. Actually, it was all of my early twenties. With that being said, I was accustomed to litany of rules and for those of you that know me know that rules and I don't always see eye to eye. Not that I would go out of my

way to get into any form of serious trouble, but little rebellions

here and there just to keep that age-old rebel in me alive. Want to

take a guess as to what one of these rules happened to be? If you

said anything other than keeping your hands out of your pockets

then I'm going to have to ask you beyond the realms of this fourth

wall to put this book down, get the strongest alcohol you have in

your house, and pour that shit straight into your eyes because they

obviously haven't been open enough thus far. Or drink it, either

work really. Back to the story now damnit. Due to this rule, for

those of you still having a hard time grasping what's coming next,

I was sure to break it all the damn time without putting myself in

any form of real troubles way. Thing is, I never noticed how often

I used to stand with my hands in my pockets before I was in the

military and let me tell you, it was a fuck ton because after two

months of basic training and being rewired to not put them mitts

back in their holster homes breaking that rule for the first time was

like a recovering crack addict's bender after years of sobriety. I mean those bitches were back in there like nobody's business. Funniest part of this whole story is that it's not going to turn into some cliché story about how the military changed one small thing about me and that changed me forever, that's a conversation for another time because the military truly did a lot for this ole sap. The way I began my conversation with this friend of mine while we were on that two-hour drive was with body language and next thing I was remembering a video I had watched years ago, I truly wish I remembered what that fucker was called but its name has escaped me for the rest of my foreseeable future, the point stuck with me though. This video, discussing body language, hit on the importance to not only the people around you but to your emotional demeanor towards yourself. Of course, my first thought, "who the actual fuck does this dude think he is?", quickly shot across my tongue as he moved right into how you should never keep your hands in your pockets during social events. Me having been someone to constantly keep my hands in my pockets unless to put a drink to my face, participate in some form of drinking game, or to constantly check the phone I had grown an umbilical cord for had a hard time understanding this. He went on into detail about how by doing this we shut ourselves in and clench ourselves up, we close ourselves to the social interaction and make us less approachable than we probably wanted to be. I thought that over for so long, longer than I probably should have. All the way back to parties from a futureless past. I looked at all the times that I shut myself into a phone instead of those who I could have spent that moment with. Don't worry, I still had plenty of good moments but I just couldn't shake that shit because I always felt myself to be such a social and confident person. Quickly understanding that I was only social and confident when I was with the people I knew or that I was comfortable with. The next gathering of debauchery we had where I knew less than the majority of people I gave this hands out of your pockets thing a go. This very well could have been some stupid placebo based action that I fell for, but it worked for me, fake or not. It's been damn near 7 years since I've seen that video and it's still stuck with me. Now the only times you see my ass with hands in my pockets are when it's cold or when I'm still

trying to be a little bit rebellious for no reason.

- M.H.

13 May 2019

      I constantly struggle in the world of procrastination and I'm more than positive that I am not alone in this dilemma. Is it truly an issue though, if we constantly get the required things done in a professional manner? What I struggle with most, is school work. Personally, I hate school but I love the ideals of education and as you can see that can be quite controversial. There are so many important things that I have learned within the walls of learning institutions but at the same time there are mountains and mountains of things that I have wasted well earned money on that either never applied to my life beyond that classroom or became obsolete in itself later on. I'm by no fucking means a genius in any fashion of the term, about as average as they come really. However, I'm constantly having to look at the flawed education, mind you this is simply an opinion of a slightly but not highly educated blabbering drunk, system that we constantly rave about. I feel that the era of standardized tests and generalized education is quickly coming to an end, especially as we watch school system after school system cut off the use of creativity in any form. I personally feel that we need to spend more time focusing on more things that matter in this world. While certain matters of general education and, to myself, history are incredibly important, we are missing out on so many other things that should be considered general education as well. At least when we are young enough to truly absorb the information. Let's start with how important it is to be a decent fucking person in this shit world we keep blindly driving through. I'm no fucking saint, but I would like to imagine that I've held some form of wings for some throughout my years thus far. I don't expect some kind of perfect utopian bullshit, but at least an idea of a world where we have a better understanding of knowing how to enjoy and understand difference between people. Don't get me wrong, I still fully side with the idea that if someone needs their ass kicked that the ass kicking is welcome as long as warranted, but buy them a fucking beer when all is said and done. Then shake their hand. No more of this stabbing and shooting in disputes. Now, that may have come off as an anti-second amendment style statement and that's where you're completely wrong. This ole fuck head is a giant supporter of the right to bear arms and own fire arms of my own. Mostly for protection of myself and my future family. I just don't stand behind the ideas of unnecessary shootings that can be solved with a beer and a handshake. Let's teach our kids what it is to be a good and strong person. Let's teach them that it's more than okay to be different. It's incredible to be creative and that no one can take their passion from them unless they let someone. Let's take the time to teach them that not everyone is meant to be academically advanced and that it is absolutely okay. Encourage the ways of education but not through standardized bullshit, rather a form of growth both intellectually and spiritually. Fuck, this is the most like a "hippy" I have ever felt I sounded like in my life. I have my own personal qualms with the education system I grew up in. It was not a bad one, but we can do much better. I was lucky enough to have educators and mentors that constantly promoted my creative side, but I also had some that went against it and focused more on their own political agenda as opposed to the unbiased information they were supposed to be

teaching. So, to tie back into how I struggle with procrastination, I

literally just finished writing a final paper that was due today. I

didn't start it until today. Talk about small school styled rebellions,

but I guess I'll have that education piece of paper because of it.

- M.H.

15 May 2019

Something I have always found odd about myself is the way I react with distractions while I am trying to focus. It's not even really my reaction to them, but I couldn't think of a better way to put it because I feel like I'm so different from a "typical" person when it comes to distractions. Where most are generally lost in entire trains of thought from another form of background noise, I absolutely fucking thrive. Seriously, at times I feel like I can't even function, at least at the rate I do, without the sounds of music or an easy to watch T.V series. Music is the big one though. There have to be more like me out there because I'm literally sitting here typing out this page while blasting a new band from my home town that I have utterly failed to listen to so far. It's as if the white noise, such a horrible way to put it because it's always music that I enjoy, makes a portion of my mind focus on the sound so the other half can focus on the task at hand. Just goes to show that some brains simply never stop and that is not supposed to be some half-witted attempt at making my ass sound intelligent.

Think I took care of that with how choppy this segment has come out so far anyways, but you never know. Sometimes, I feel like I can't get my brain to stop, it's the worst at night. There are constantly songs playing, new songs forming, memories that skipped the instructions on the stop button, and a constant black out of words that are just wishing to be written down. When I was first getting into writing I would take sticky notes or receipt paper from my place of work and quickly jot down the words as the came to me. This was both releasing and frustrating at the same time as I would take them home and try to finish an idea whose emotion had been lost to the moment it was written. When I had the chance, I would type these little brief couplets into my phone and sometimes whole poems. The memo app on my phone was pretty much a forest and a graveyard for ideas that I had planted and tried to bring about perfectly. However, this became a struggle later on as I entered into more professional lines of work. As the moments on my phone were constantly taken for moments I was choosing to ignore work and to message others when in fact they were simply five minutes of me pouring out what was in my head and in my heart simply so that I could focus on my work. Although, I can completely understand the perception of the whole thing and to those employers and supervisors that thought I was disrespecting them and their time, I whole heartedly apologies. But this is the only apology you're getting for my odd antics.

We live in this age where a lost phone is a life sentence for the moments you have to go without it. While I was originally a victim to the same addiction known by my fellow peers, I found a different reason to feel empty at the loss of a phone. I think back to any phone I've lost and I hope that whoever finds it, can not only understand and enjoy all of the memos of written gibberish I've constantly littered my Instagram and books with but also steers quite clear of the years of weird ass pictures I've collected.

- M.H.

22 May 2019

Since the day that I officially started working on this little pile of paper and ink, I have been making small notes here and there about certain things that might be good topics to write about. Sometimes it's simply a word and other times I try to capture the moment in a few more than that if I can, but here again I set out with one thing in mind and feel that I can't perfectly capture the moment I remembered. The worst part of it all, is that in this exact moment, I thought that I had found something new to go touch on but instead I'm fumbling around words and thinking far too much about the movie I turned on. Been trying to numb a little more of the things we call physical senses in order to bring out more of the inner senses. I know it sounds ridiculous, but maybe the films of choice have been that insight for me lately. Moving pictures of musicians and writers who constantly sought after inner peace through outer expression and found themselves constantly turning to other forms of, what we'll say, clarity. I fall under the drinking side of that table and write every emotion that's shined through each of the whiskey bottles. Maybe it's our form of muse from the times we thought we found one but were simply tricked again. I remember the last time someone called themselves my muse, took that shit to heart actually. She even put it into poet form to try and connect with me better. Fuck, if that wasn't the biggest lie I have ever believed. So, we keep our lives in bottles and write them on lines when the time is right. Well, let's be real about it, it's never when the time is right (the amount of times I just misspelled "right" with "write" before finally reviewing this is insane). I've made a lot of mistakes with my life, a lot of them occurred while trying to numb myself to the things that caused me to be afraid of this physical world. But, at the same time I've created things that I could have never imagined coming from this ole drunken fuck. I never said that any of it was good, but it was about as real as it could get. Be ready for poorly written poems about broken hearts and too many phone calls, because that's just how I reach out in the moments I'm numb and alone.

- M.H.

2 June 2019

I've got to say, sitting upright in bed sober, while writing this feels odd. But I had to get the words out of my blood. See, that's what I've been stuck on tonight. In this age of internet and social media, sharing our music, our writing, our art has never been easier. The worst part is I can taste the hypocrisy as I say I feel it's caused it all to lose its authenticity. I use social media to share my work but I'll be damned if those fifteen minutes of fame I so rarely get are what defines why I do it. Some of us simply have to get the words out because the thing that waits for us if we don't is a scary thing. I think maybe that's why we drink so much; it either allows us to get it all out in ease or helps us to hide from the words constantly cutting themselves into our bodies with pens. I've heard the idea of how you would look if the words you spoke showed on your skin, but what about those that write their hearts in pages? Will their skin simply show as ink black, or a withered picture of a broken heart? Life's not always rainbows and sunshine and that's why I think writers like us exist. To write about why we wish.

\- M.H.

21 June 2019

The amount of times that I've heard the phrase "everything is temporary" has found its own way of being counted. It's called an ironic headache. Today, while browsing through the poetic additives to the writing world that is Instagram, I think I read that phrase at least four or five different times within a span of three hours. Each time just feeling both a melancholy that was meant for the phrase itself and a minor distaste at the thought of its actual meaning to us. It truly got my brain churning as to what I truly think about the phrase, especially after reading it the second time through. While I cannot disagree that it is in-fact a fact in itself, I think we are overlooking the hanging shadow that is the temporary time we have on this world. Relationships, thoughts, fuck beers, and even life are temporary and that's the whole premise of this phrase. Is it not? What I think about, every time I read or think about it, is that if everything is temporary then what am I doing to make and find things that are going to feel timeless? What are the things in our lives that even on the worst days, when every writer just wants to sit back and stab out the words "EVERYTHING IS TEMPORARY" into their notebooks, that make us think, "you know what, I know this will end someday but it makes me feel complete forever"? That's a good question to ask ourselves. Something that I can't perfectly answer myself, yet here I am typing down pages for a pile of trees that I hope to live passed the limits of time. So, yes, my time is temporary and everything in this world is in-fact temporary because we are simply that, temporary, but I'll be damned if my temporary time here doesn't feel like the perfect forever for me.

- M.H.

22 June 2019

I wonder, if by the pages you've read so far, if you can gather what my position is on tattoos. A topic that has been quite controversial, more so in the time of my generation as they became more and more common amongst the modern-day employee and less the biker gang taboo of the past. If for some reason, you have deluded yourself into thinking that I stand on the negative side of ink's permanence to the skin, then I'm sorry, well not that sorry, to say you're quite fucking wrong. I've had this strange affinity for tattoos, much like I did with cigarettes, since I was of a young age. Something about different images scattered across your body making your skin gleam like a weathered piece of history and art. Though my incredibly catholic family saw things differently, and I think even scorned at the idea of tattoos on the body made perfect by God. That was simply my adolescent idea for why I loved tattoos so much until it came time for me to get my first.

Eighteen, the legal age to stab needles into your skin that would leave images that lasted forever. I remember the experience perfectly as being the worst tattoo experience of my entire life. Walked in with this idea of an Irish styled crucifix, with the Celtic knots and Irish blessing on it and everything. I know, how fucking basic white boy could I have possibly been? I ended up leaving with the first line of the Irish blessing stitched across my chest in what felt like eternity, but in reality, only took thirty minutes. Again with the douchy white guy stereotypes, but I was proud of what I had done and I felt like a man. To me, this tattoo felt like a connection the Irish part of my family that I so full of pride expressed and continue to. So, when it comes to tattoos I find a certain sense of artistic and degenerate connections of the heart. I took this idea of the heart and ran with it, each of my tattoos is either a symbolic representation of an accomplishment I have made that was important to me or defined me as a person, or has ties to family and friends who I hold dearer than life itself. While I support the whole argument of it's your body, decorate it how you see fit. I don't see myself getting too many spur of the moment tattoos that have little to know meaning for me. I constantly struggle to think of something symbolic to represent the accomplishments I wish to cover my body in as is. Each one of the books I've published have their own tattoos, as well as a couple of my biggest influences with my writing and music. I'm sure in sometime, once this book is set in front of you bound in some form of decorative skin that I spent minutes to fabricate, I'll have another piece linked to my skin and heart for eternity to represent it. To those of you reading this that are still on the fence on whether or not they should get tattoos or not remember this, tattoos don't define who you are as a person but simply help you show the type of person you've worked so hard to become.

- M.H.

3 July 2019

Originally dated this page 27 June, my birthday, but after typing out a whole paragraph of what I thought would have been a thoroughly enjoyable addition to this project just came off so sappy and annoying to me, and I'm the one that wrote it. My twenty-fifth birthday, a day I spent between work, napping, and quite honestly not a damn thing else. I think it was the first birthday, in quite some time, that I've spent without a drink. It felt strange but at the same time a little more relaxing. My body probably needed the break. Not that I've been abusing my body too much you judgmental fucks. That weekend however was one for the books indeed. It wasn't necessarily crazy in a sense that I partied any more than I usually would on a weekend out here in Europe, but it had this strange bitter after taste of disputes between the physical and mental that I tried to wash away in the way of alcoholic homilies.

My friends will be the first to tell you that I have this weird knack for always wanting to be the last one standing on a night out.

To most, that may come off as a strange, yet in a world so used to it, normal dependence on alcohol and being unable to stop. But, that just isn't it for me. I love the random interactions, the different people that I get to meet, and the experiences that I hope to remember. With that being said, I remember that the last bar I went to I had a sudden moment of drunken euphoria. I thought about how much we don't appreciate moments for what they have to offer, experience and all. Then, I next thought about what things that I have yet to experience for myself simply out of interest. After befriending a man sitting at this new gin bar and sharing a couple drinks and conversations about normal drunken topics of the night I told him my interest in sleeping by myself in a park for a night, just so I can say to myself that I tried it. Once I decided I've had my final drink for the night I walked over to my favorite late night food stand with this odd drunken skip in my step. After making my way with a beer and a box of food I realized the closest park was not a walking feat I was wanting to complete at four in the morning. Stumbled upon a bush, looked like a nice bush that could be maybe into a makeshift bed and enough cover to hide me from the world around me that wouldn't understand what I was trying to accomplish without thinking I was beyond this worlds idea of sanity. Set my food upon what I called a "shelf" within the bushes and enjoyed the remnants of my beer before drifting off to what would become one of the most satisfying naps of my life. A few hours later I woke up, disposed of my trash, because apparently, I care about my environment and walked on back to my friend's house roughly 10 minutes up the road. That walk truly allowed me to reflect on what I had just done, as I let music play from my phone taking in the morning air and the early events of opening shops. It allowed me to see that I haven't done something simply out of curiosity, something simply for me in far too long. I think that was the first time I felt close to that old me that I knew and loved a couple years back. Something as stupid as sleeping in a bush because I wanted to really put a different spin on where my head had been at for as long as I can remember now. It's amazing the things that help us to feel like us, like we belong again.

- M.H.

7 July 2019

I've been reading a lot of Bukowski lately, mostly the series he wrote about his early life as a character named Henry. I think the reason I chose to really start getting more into his writing, now that I'm finally jumping back on the reading wagon again, is because of how many times other people have told me my writing is so similar to his. As a young writer, and really still to this day, I find that to be quite the compliment but realized I had only read a handful of poems and quotes of his that more than caught my fancy. The first thing that slapped me right in the face was his voice of what comes off as pure disgust with what the world around him is. That and his incredible drinking habits that, quite frankly, made me feel better about my own. And that's really what got me thinking about this page I'm currently set in front of this computer for. In fact, I've been in such deep thought about it the past twelve hours that I'm having a hard time finding the right words to say. His life literally revolved around the bottle and I wondered if that's what everyone thought when they read anything that I've written. While I'm not necessarily opposed to that sort of atmosphere around my writing it sat with me funny because I looked at the way this man was constantly drinking. In a world where he felt alone, that he wasn't similar to anyone, and the cheap whiskey or wine was the only thing that helped cope with that ideal. In that however, is where I found my similarities and maybe that's why I received the number of comparisons between our writing. Talked about it before and I'll probably talk about it again, it just has this way of releasing us from the chains we feel around ourselves as we work our way through each day. I do not typically drink during the weekdays like him however, but I understand. It's this toxic yet invigorating super power that we have where we can turn off the world around us at the turn of a bottle top and just empty everything we are onto paper through a bottled filter. Everyone's had their share of bad nights due to alcohol, but I can think of so many great ones I had because of it. I wonder if he was truly like me though, one second you're on top of the world and the next it just hits you. Loneliness, and there's nothing you can do about it after your lips have touched that precious substance one too many times. I guess that's why they call it a depressant and tell you not to drink alone, you'll end up years deep on memories scouring your phone calling everyone you know and miss. It's become my weekend ritual, end up the last one awake because your brain just won't turn off and calling everyone back home halfway across the world. Maybe that's what writers are running from when they turn to the bottle and feel imprisoned by words, I think we're all just running from loneliness.

- M.H.

11 July 2019

I once used to be incredibly involved in the world of online writing, between writing pages I had on certain apps or websites. Every hour or so I would pull up the feed and scroll through reading what the rest of that community had to share that day. I found a lot of inspiration and motivation from rummaging through these works of art. Something I got away from in the past year or so now. There was always one thing that bothered me deep down every time I did this though and possibly why I stepped away from being as involved as I was. There were simply too many "try hards" no matter where you looked. And I know how conceited that sounds, in fact it's difficult for me to even write it out without a sense of bullshit sitting heavy on my mind. Who am I to say that anyways? I'm by no means some expert writer that knows everything if anything about the subject. It was just this feeling I would get when reading certain pieces, words forced into sentences that simply didn't flow right, a lack of actual emotion, and this overbearing disgust of trying to do too much in so little time. For all I know, they could feel the very same as me when reading something I've written. Fuck, I'm sure there are words that make me sound no better than some child first discovering the word "supercalifragilisticexpialidocious". In fact, before I ever started sharing my writing with the world I used to keep a dictionary app on my phone and would try to incorporate the word of the day into something, just to better understand the word and to maybe make myself feel better about my own intelligence. I think the one thing that set myself apart from everyone else in these communities is that they were doing it to fit in, whereas I was just writing to write, because I needed to write. Every page that had my signature also bore the emotions that I had brought to that lined battle ground. This has turned into quite the ramble and I can't even fully remember where exactly I was heading with this, but I think what's important about something, whether you're the reader or the writer, is to feel some type of real emotion in the words. No matter their presentation, their pattern. The right words are going to make you feel something, good or bad, and their always signed in blood.

Censillaphobia, look that one up. My favorite forced word that I signed my name to more than once.

- M.H.

15 July 2019

I had the hardest time deciding whether or not to write down this date or wait the fifteen minutes for it to be the sixteenth. Obviously, we can all see what my final decision was. What a strange intro for a page but would this really be a book by me if it wasn't a little strange in nature? For those who don't know me, the answer is, absolutely fucking not. Originally, I had one topic picked out to write about the other night, but I was caught up in travel for work and found myself quite literally scrubbing my phone screen to make sure half of the topics I wrote down were real. Funny thing, is I think the one I was set out to write about before the chaos of travel was, "Are you pissed when the sandwich is gone, or satisfied?". That is one hundred and fifty percent a sprinkle of ole Mike Hipp written all over it and not a lie. Even says that I originally wrote it down on the seventh of July. While the whole sentence itself starts off so incredibly odd, I think that I can attempt to decipher what I'm guessing was some moment of drunken euphoria for all of us. It seems pretty straight forward, I was curious if you assholes were content with something you gorged yourselves with or would you become a glutton for your own satisfaction? Let's be real, most of my ideals aren't that metaphorical, as much as I'd like them to be at least. So, if you're having a hard time grasping this, maybe you're one of those people in question. Can we not be satisfied for one second? Just take a look around us and just enjoy what we have. I'm about as big of a mixture between pessimistic and optimistic as anyone could ever hope to be and I still take moments every so often to just look around and fall back in love with the things around me. Don't get me wrong, I definitely have my bad times, horrible fucking times where I can't escape my own head, but I always find something to keep me anchored to this Earth. And if you know me, you know how much I cringed as I typed out that last sentence, but it's simply a fact. The last time I truly took a moment to sit back and just fall back in love with the world itself was last week. That was the first time I had done it moderately sober in a long time at least. I went to a concert for the first time in months, but this was no ordinary concert. This was my favorite bands concert, my favorite band that happens to be from the same home town as me that I got to meet out back and engage in awesome conversation about music and mutual friends before they took off on the rest of their European tour. While my only fanboy moment to date was an interesting event, that wasn't the moment I was talking about. At least every thirty-minutes or so, at every show I go to, I turn around and look at the crowd and just enjoy the fact that we're all joined together for this one thing and in this one time. A time where differences in social status, culture, or politics can affect us. A time where we can all just simply fall in love with a moment we will never forget, even if we were to die tomorrow. Those are the moments I fall in love with and those are the moments I hope to keep living for in this life. The simple ones, gathered with all of my fellow drunken degenerates screaming our favorite songs that saved our lives.

- M.H.

19 July 2019

Even though I've been writing this bad boy quite consistently there are times where I forget whether or not I've written about one thing or another. I would like to say I apologize for this next one if I've written about it before, but truly I don't give a fuck. You chose to pick it up, so enjoy it.

Letters, when's the last time you wrote one? I bet it's longer than you would ever like to admit. Personally, I love letters. Not just because I love writing but because I love the idea of sitting down and taking time to write something out for one individual person. In a time where we can get a message in seconds, the thought of waiting a week or two becomes more intimate and I love every second of it. Every person I call close or girl I have ever found true interest in, I always ask for an address or provide mine. It's a disappearing art. Not just the art of writing, but the idea of intimacy in pages. When was the last time you received a piece of paper that was meant only for you? I've written too many and it's always been an interesting experience to see who actual returns the favor. More times than not, it doesn't happen. But I can think of many letters I wrote to certain people where I wrote a poem on the spot that I wished to get back because it was something I was truly proud of but at the time meant only for them. In a world where we're so lost behind phone screens, we forget the importance of face to face communication and because of that we forget the lessons that written letters used to teach us. Patience. So, next time you go away, whether its fifteen minutes or fifteen hours, start writing them letters. It means a hell of a lot more than the occasional text message I promise. A written letter is an extension of your hand and there's work involved with it, and to me, that's fucking beautiful. Write me letters about bad days and good days all together. Tell me about why you cried and what made you smile. Use those words you learned as a child and run them through an envelope. Just make sure you sign it with love like I always do.

- M.H.

21 July 2019

Was going to make my way through another one of my listed topics, but this recent experience was far too interesting for me not to mention. For those that don't know me in the flesh, I am quite into tattoos and have a fair amount of them. With that said, I like to get at least one in every new place I go but sometimes there just isn't enough time. This most recent one that I got yesterday was in Poland and quite the adventure all together. The night prior I spent between Harry Potter movie binging with my coworkers and partaking in the few "distinguished" alcohol consuming establishments in the small town we are staying in. Originally, I had intent of going to bed early so as to arrive early to my appointment well rested and hydrated. Well, can you guess that just didn't happen? I mean, why else would I be writing about it right now if it did? After our round about the bars in the town we returned to the hotel which has a bar open twenty-four hours a day. After a few more beers and some good ole Polish vodka myself and another decided we were in need of some sustenance of the tobacco kind and quickly took off for the nearest gas station to fulfill this late-night craving. What was supposed to be a hour long, at the most journey, quickly turned from 0300 in the morning to 0830 coming back for the hotels free breakfast. On the way, back I remembered a shortcut back to the hotel and offered it up as a suggestion, it took us through a park that I had drank in with another friend the last time I was in town. Quickly realizing I didn't remember the exact route through this bad boy, we came across a group of ponds and in the early light of the morning it's amazing how beautiful and peaceful something as simple as a pond full of ducks and be. For hours, we sat there talking about life, talking about our passions, what's most dear to our hearts, and of course most importantly music. Conversations like this I can take part in for days on end, it's something I live for. So, of course even though the clock was ticking on my soon to happen tattoo appointment I could help but indulge on this addiction of conversation. After finally realizing what time it was we headed back to the hotel so as to grab that delicious free breakfast I mentioned and gather the last remaining couple of hours I could manage. After fighting with myself as to whether or not I should just stay up or take a quick nap I eventually just drifted off and awoke a solid hour late for my appointment. Frantically rushing into the shower nearly falling and cracking my head on the way out the door I rushed off to the tattoo shop as quickly as my feet could possibly move without looking like so ridiculous freak sprinting through the Polish streets in the morning. After finally making it there and quickly apologizing as many times as possible making up whatever excuse I could so as not to lose my appointment the artist acted as if nothing had happened and greeted me openly. Maybe it was the language barrier, but I guess we'll never know. Knocked out the appointment with no issues and left incredibly satisfied with the piece hoping I didn't completely reek of alcohol from the night before. To celebrate myself I went to the local pierogi spot and quickly entered into a sweating fit of hangover. I'm not sure what I was supposed to grasp from this experience but I have always felt that great conversations with others about what they love most will always be more important than something as material as a tattoo and healthy sleep. I don't think I would have been able to reschedule that appointment since we were leaving the next week but I would have happily walked away from this experience with a smile because I left it with a new friend who probably hadn't felt safe with venting about himself and his heart in a long time. Don't ever forget how important the people around you are.

- M.H.

29 July 2019

I'll let you guess at what a typical Saturday morning looks like for me, but let me tell you this last one was something right in line with different. Usually, I find myself out on a Friday evening leaving me to sleep through a majority of the next morning. As I'm sure you can gather this far, that was not the case this particular Saturday. Quite annoyed I woke up far too early and could not find the path back to back to a peaceful slumber, I blame the ridiculous European heat due to the LACK OF AIR CONDITIONING! After a couple hours of staring at phone screens and wishing the sounds of T.V. shows could put me back to sleep, I finally got up and looked from my balcony at my yard in disgust as I hadn't groomed that poor bastard in weeks. I'm sure there are many others like myself that enjoy the peace and solitude of lawn work. Pop some headphones in, a smoke or tight lip of chew, and away you go.

I actually think up a majority of my writing topics and song ideas while chopping away the overgrown grass and weeds. But what hit me hardest was listening to music and finding myself revisiting a topic I failed to finish discussing within the first couple of pages. The way different songs can make you time travel back to the times you assimilate with each note. I've always had a remarkably, at least to me, precise memory and I wonder if the reason is because I group moments that meant something to me with songs that breathe like me. It's weird, but I can remember things as odd as my sixth-grade crush when I listen to the old pop emo bands of the time, or the shirt an old high school fling wore the first time we met. I can remember all of the fun and degenerate things I did with friends while blasting the sounds of one of our favorite, now dead, rappers. Moments lost in pure euphoria after coming down from a weekend of partying with a close friend that I haven't seen in years. It's a trait that I truly love about myself, being able to remember things and every emotion I felt around them just because of a few songs that meant so much to me. I say I love it, but I also see it as a curse on the nights that I can't get out of my head. For someone that has always had a love for the ways of music and what it can be for every person individually, I never thought favorite songs could betray my mental stability, but it's happened more times than I'd like to even count. Like I said, I remember everything down to raw feelings of the moment when I think about it. That means the times I wish I could forget have this strange way of flirting with the few remaining bricks between the walls of past and growth. Bricks I made with the leftovers of many bottles, the tar of a few burnt lungs, and decades worth of regrets for what's still considered a short life thus far. Problem is that when the right song hits, it's like the cement made from that just falls apart and I'm right back where I started. In the past but cutting new words into notebooks to try and get back.

Music is my best friend and even when it hurts, it's still there for me as much now as it was then. I think what I'm really hoping to accomplish with all of these things I play with, is to make something that someone remembers the good things to.

- M.H.

10 August 2019

Let's talk about writing for a minute here. Well, not like you really have a choice, but I guess if you're really that turned off by talking about writing in a book that took quite a bit of writing to create then maybe you should just skip these next few pages or simply set the book down and walk away now. I caught myself mid thought earlier thinking about why it is that writers do what they do and what really got them into it. Is it out of need for expression, maybe fear of personal expression, or they are simply just gods literary gift to the damned world and they just bless the pages they pull out of their ass? In my experience, I came into writing by accident. As cliché as that could possibly sound, but I really came into writing by accident. Back in the days of the idea child a few of my friends and I came up with. That's right, we were all thinking it, a good ole death metal band. I was going to do lead vocals and play bass. It was truly just an empty dream that we used in talks of hope on what our lives could be, it was fun even though we never practiced and I never learned how to play the bass. That is exactly where it all started though, I would write up the lyrics for our songs. Full of blood, death, decapitation, and a whole lot of religion. Oh, did I forget to mention we were a Christian death metal band? Oops, yeah that was the path this old drunk was on at a young age. I can remember writing those lyrics, fuck, I still have them in a notebook somewhere that has this weird color to it now from the time a cheap bottle of whiskey spilled and soiled all the pages. You can still see the chicken scratch notes my buddy gave me because he was the almighty lyricist at the time, we really had no idea what we were doing but it was fun and I loved every second of it. It was my first time being able to just say whatever I wanted to in a place that could be appreciated. A black spiral notebook filled with a mixture of blue and black ink that felt more like blood to me.

As I said before, the band never really made it anywhere, but what can a group of Christian degenerates expect of a band that never practiced and straight up didn't even have the instruments? After that was when I really started to branch out with my writing, at first it felt like it no longer had a purpose but then I started getting this feeling every time I would write something new. It was almost like I was leaving a piece of me with every word I put down. Ink smudges and cramped hands became my trophies and I just kept delving deeper and deeper into the ideas of traditional rhyming couplets and, as we can all see, later saying fuck that shit and just throwing together whatever style of words I wanted. I really wish I would have dated these things back then but as they say hind sight is quite a bitch. I'm actually reading through the second notebook I ever filled up with writing right now and I think it's necessary to share it here just so we can all laugh together at the place I was with writing back then.

"I never wrote these poems I bled them,
From a heart that was broke in seven.
Since these are my secret thoughts,
The quiet wars that I fought.
I wasn't twisted by just you,

Surely it came from a few.

Or rather was I destructive from the start?

Simply born to fall apart.

Because of the years the only gift I've seen,

Just happens to be the one of my dreams.

My gift is these lines

That are constructed from metaphorical rhymes.

I used to pray the battle come easy,

But now I beg it to see me.

Every little thrash against this heart

Just gives my weapons more power to start.

So if I must continue to feel the whip

I won't pray for it to end quick.

I'll put my trust in my Lord

Since he has given me my sword.

I'll write about the venom you spit

Even your little perfect fits.

At least I hide my rage

And keep it locked in a secret cage.

Where you just let your mouth run,

Trust me, its not attractive hun."

Well how about that for a trip down memory lane. The first page of the notebook at that. No use of drinking or smoking metaphors and still a casual use of poor grammar, though it looks as though back then I was even worse. We've made progress, I count that as a score in my corner at least. It's just so strange to look back and read all of these and remember how different my world was back then, each piece just brings back so many memories. It's like my heart is connecting with the pieces I left on those lines every time I read it and that's what I love so much about writing. So, this is going to keep going because while I was flipping through this particular notebook, I found a piece that was actually signed and dated from back in 2012. Better known as the time I was super into writing vivid descriptions of certain images or things I saw in that moment. Without further ado, heres a clip

from the brain of Mike Hipp dating 10 May 2012,

"For what must be the first time in my life I can put that

damned device of communication away. Just sit back put my

headphones in and stare out the window. Watching as the sun

reflects calmly off the billion blades of grass, swaying to and fro in

a sweet little dance. I can feel the breeze against my face and feel

the touch and soothing graze of those who have left me. Even if the

world were to end today honestly I can say I'm ready, I just sit in

silence creeping on the world outside with the joyful of grins.

Holding back tears from the sudden epitome *(super misspelled this*

word) of the beauty around me. Everything that was so good I

casted aside and only pictured the darkness, the demons, the hate

in everything. I let my past consume me and never let myself grow

into the man I should be with a smile upon my face. I pledge and I

pray that I become that man I'm destined to be and not focus on what its I want *(verbatim how I wrote it back then)* or even what I need, just be happy and let the good follow shortly behind."

Nothing has really change between now and then really, that's coming up on eight years ago now and I can say that I still fail on that whole focusing on the past part. Funny thing, is that I can still see the window I was looking out of in the computer lab between the classrooms of two of my favorite teachers. This memory of mine is surely something, but writing myself into pages has this magical effect on a moment in making it eternal. As far as becoming the man I was supposed to be, who fucking knows, I guess that's on the rest of you to decide. You're all the ones that have to deal with my debatured ass. Yes, I just made that word up. Never the less, this was a great look back and the old pieces I shed of myself back then.

- M.H.

28 August 2019

I've been going back and forth for nearly a week now on whether or not to write about this but I'm finally saying fuck it. As I'm sure you've gathered this far, music is quite an important part of my life and from an early age I was introduced to some of the greatest music to ever be written by my dad. In fact, if we look back to some of my earliest proclamations as to what I wanted to be when I grew up, almost every time you'd hear me say a firefighter, like my father, or a rock star. I'm sure batman was another occupation I was quite interested in as well, but that's beside the point.

Music is something I actively went after starting from a young age, though neither of my parents played instruments as I grew up, I was always fascinated at the way music was made and of course the sound of the guitar, as I'm sure most were that grew up on classic rock like I did. My first venture into playing an instrument however, was the saxophone in the school band. It always fascinated me but I hated to practice, I always wanted to learn the songs as we practiced at school. I became quite proficient in forging my mother's initials when it came to practice minutes, which was our homework for band. School band truly wasn't that big of an interest to me but when I was playing I loved every second of it. I did that for about 5 years and to this day I'm unsure as to what would happen if I picked up a saxophone again.

On my thirteenth birthday, after constructing my own make-shift guitar neck from string and cardboard to try and teach myself how to play, I had convinced my parents to let me buy my first guitar with the birthday money I had collected and quickly learned that I sucked the second I got it home. Within thirty-minutes of trying to figure out how to tune the damn thing, I snapped a string and the fucking thing nearly took my eye out scaring me for life on venturing into the world of crazy tunings for fear of snapping one of those bad boys again. Taught myself a few chords and played them horribly all the time while taking pictures to show off just how cool I was with my guitar. But I loved it. The challenge of it all, knowing that I really wasn't any good, but that satisfaction I felt throughout my whole being when I played it. Like I said though, I wasn't very good, so I did not put in the work I should have when it came to learning this instrument and so I just sat in the realms of mediocre for the next couple years. Learning chords and tabs here and there, but nothing all that impressive. Fast-forward to my first year of community college, a time that I dreaded and suffered through but scheduled myself a guitar class for an elective credit. I did far better than I ever expected in this classical guitar class, still nowhere beyond the terms of mediocre, but more confident. The next year, I finally tried a couple lessons, they lasted maybe a month or two, once a week. The only thing we really did at these lessons was jam together and the fact that I was able to do that with another musician who was considered a professional in the local area was one of the biggest accomplishments of my life.

It took me until I was stationed in Oklahoma, at the age of twenty-one to finally try my hand at songs where I sing and play together. I know I sucked, I sucked bad, but it was so gratifying and I can't even begin to explain what I felt every time something I felt deep down came out in song. I had friends that would tell me I wasn't really all that great but they were impressed because they never expected anything like that from me. I pushed those comments off and continued writing songs that I still play to this day until a very important significant other in my life told me that I wasn't anything special at the guitar, my voice wasn't truly all that great, but my writing was something that put me beyond most people my caliber. Which, remember, wasn't all that high to begin with. Hearing her say those things and constantly comparing me to her "famous" musician friends really did a number on me, but I was determined to keep writing music. So, I adapted a style that was similar to bands I liked, I would loop a guitar part and speak some of my poetry over it, then play solo styled guitar parts in-between. I fucking loved every second of it and eventually just kept writing songs in both formats after I accepted that I wasn't doing this music thing to be good, I was never doing it to be famous, I was doing it to be a support system for anyone that related to it. To be there for anyone that had ever felt the same way I had when I wrote the songs. About a year after we went our separate ways, I finally took some audio from my online video channel and turned it into two albums which I posted on a streaming website. I've started playing shows, accumulating more friends in the music scene, and fans that have walked up to me after small shows or open mics to tell me how much they felt the emotion in my music. I guess what I was trying to accomplish with this piece, was to convince myself and everyone else, that no matter what anyone says to you, if you have a dream go fucking get it and don't let anyone stop you. Mines still growing every single day and I never plan to stop.

- M.H.

11 September 2019

First and foremost, let's talk about how you should never write down a book topic idea while you've been drinking. Who in the fuck is going to remember what the "Steve Irwin of alcohol" means? I wrote that idea down in my phone on 19 July, if you're able to read the date at the top of this page then I'm sure we can deduce that it's been quite some time since I knew what I was talking about with this one. Truly can't even explain how I came across this idea originally but something hit me just now and it seems we're just going to have to dive deeper into it before it drives me insane.

At the time, and remember this is purely guessing, I think I was thinking of different kinds of alcohol as their own forms of wild animals and me being a decently big fan of Steve Irwin felt it necessary to deem myself an expert in that field as he was with animals. From what drink you need for a relaxed night, one where you're trying to forget the existence of the day you're currently in, one to bring that weak ass stomach of yours back to life after some raunchy food, and of course the perfect escape plan from any and every hangover. Don't get me wrong, this sounds horrible, but I'm pretty sure at this point I have a degree from drinking my problems away but found my doctorate in moderated drinking that is neither sloppy nor too harmful to the insides, so maybe you should take a listen. But, in the facts of health, definitely consult a real doctor. Remember, I'm just a fun drunk with a keyboard and a talent with pens. On top of my vast knowledge in all things alcoholic, I also have this strange talent for finding people that seem to be just wishing to give away free drinks and becoming their new best friend for the night. In fact, there are times I will wander off on my own from my group of friends and come back with a free case of beer and a few new friends. I truly don't know what it is, maybe I get it from my family, this ability to enter any situation and befriend someone that I had never met before and continue to be friends with them after they hooked me up with some more drinks or smokes. If you are one of those friends, sorry bud but at this point you should know better with me because as with any friend I always keep in touch. I'm sure everyone of the friends, long-term or whom I met one of those nights and kept in touch with, has their own stories of nights I've taken them on a wilderness adventure of the drinking kind. Seems I like to keep the good times going and memories fun. So, to all friends, new and old, I look forward to our next drink and our next adventure. Hold those memories as close as you can because you know for sure I am. When I remember them that is. (I laughed when I wrote that)

- M.H.

11 September 2019

I have recently started into the world of writing by Hemingway. Started. I had not realized the first book I had bought was the library edition with every introduction ever written and reference excerpts about how long it had taken him to write the book in its entirety. I have barely gotten through four pages of the actual novel itself after reading all of the introductions. Now, before anyone goes and says I'm talking shit about this book and this work, I'm going to quickly tell you to shut the fuck up because that is the exact opposite of what I'm doing. The main thing that stuck out to me at this point was how many times Ernest went back and rewrote the ending. If I remember correctly, it was thirty-nine different endings until he finally settled on the one that made it perfect. The amount of time that it must have taken to put up thirty-nine different endings to a novel must have been astronomical, but I appreciate so much that he was simply attempting to make his work an absolute masterpiece. The reason this all stuck with me is because it made me reflect on my writing because I like to find a connection with each of the authors that truly catch my interest. But, the problem here, is that where he took all this time to perfect his masterpiece, I honestly just sit down and write away and will never edit it again. I'm afraid that once you go back and try to change something, whether it be from a poem or something long like this, that you lose the original emotions behind what drove you to write it. It takes me anywhere from five to fifteen minutes to write a poem, fifteen to thirty minutes to write something like this, and anywhere from half an hour to an hour to write a song. It made me think that maybe I don't put enough into it, but that simply can't be true. Every time I step away from pen or paper I feel as though I've lifted every bit of weight from my shoulders. Sometimes, I feel like I can finally breathe again. While I commend that man for being a perfectionist when it came to his masterpiece I'm afraid that's the one thing I can't connect with. Because to me, the best masterpieces are written in pure emotion at the right moment. That goes for everyone, not just myself. If I can feel you in those lyrics, in those pages, on those brush strokes, that's a masterpiece to me. It's going to sound cliché, but don't hold yourself to the standards of others, because your masterpiece may be their garbage; and something you thought to be absolute shit could be the best thing that has ever happened for them. Fall in love with your story, not how everyone else got to theirs.

- M.H.

23 September 2019

The pages are starting to become more spread out, and I think that really fits the purpose of this whole novel adventure. I've read so many different articles and watched my fair share of interviews about how some people just sit down and write out a novel in its entirety. The problem, is that I do the exact same thing, most of the time. If words hit my head and need to be spilled, I immediately find pen, paper, or phone to quick get them down. I'm also not that big on editing, I feel as though writing can lose its emotional presence when we edit it too much, especially for myself. You know, because I'm an illiterate fuck that makes up his own words and ways to write sentences. But, I think that's probably why I have always loved writing so much, especially this pile of parchment. I can wait for the right moment, when something just hits me and I can simply let loose and, as much as I hate it, type the fuck away on something that is hitting the heart in the moment. There's something about being able to live in a story you're telling yourself, but it's even weirder when you're actually the character of all these thoughts and stories.

I've heard a few times before that I have this distinct voice, when someone reads my writing, that can only sound like me. That's truly something I feel proud of because; well, I hope someone hears something and it's not just empty sentences set on dead trees. You have no idea how many times I just misspelled sentence while writing this, if that goes to show how well I do with "professional" writing.

I encourage everyone to start writing again, so many of us stopped. I hope everyone can find out what that voice inside their head sounds like. Mines an alcoholic with the worst case of anxiety I've ever seen. He fears the actions he hasn't done for someone else yet and drinks to try and find himself. So, I've become quite talented at understanding slurred words, broken hearts, and just why the fuck half of us are just not enough.

- M.H.

28 September 2019

Here's a topic that I've really been trying to avoid talking about within this book, but I guess there's no better place for it. Toxic relationships. I'm no expert, but then again, no one with a PhD truly is either. We all continue learning as we go about our respective fields. Just seems that mine was chosen for me. Now, I will not go into details or drop names out of respect for the people that come to mind when I think about this one and trust me, I think about it more often than I want to. It has this haunting presence in my brain that I used to wash out with far too much whiskey and days on days of sleep. There were times that I couldn't stand the idea of sleeping in my own bed, the couch was my safe haven and random T.V shows mixed with whiskey were my comfort food. Needless to say, this was a not so pretty time in my life and I struggled to crawl out of it, but here we are. I started with cleaning up my mess that had been accumulating for the past few months, started working out again, and wrote so much music that at one point my fingers bled from how many times I played through a new song just to record it perfectly the same day I wrote it. Re-discovered my love for reading and dove into the world of Bukowski like a pool without water. I forget where or when, but I read about toxic relationships causing PTSD, as a military member I hate to accept it, but it's true. There were times where I'd have flash backs of memories as I would creep around my house. Other times I woke up in cold sweats from nightmares of that person returning as if nothing had happened. See, but I will never call what was going on with me PTSD, I just simply was trying to recover and my head and my heart just simply wouldn't let me. That's the thing with us stupid writers, once we fall in love, we can never fully let it go until we find someone or something else to love equally or more. It's fucked up, but it shows in every time I write. I've kept the existence of those that have hurt me in the past right there in the present with me just from spilling blood on dead trees. Truly a scary thing to think about if you're not like us, but writing it out is exactly what we need.

Hi, I'm Mike and I'm not better yet, but if I can come this far, just imagine what you can do.

- M.H.

30 September 2019

I have had quite my fair share of adventures this past going on six years now and I may even venture to write a book about all of that debauchery one day. While I don't believe my adventures are bound for an end anytime soon, I have to say the thing I have missed the most, is my home. For those who never left good ole Grand Rapids and hate that they are "stuck" there, I'm sorry but you don't know what you're talking about. Sure, the winters are hard, we're all kind of loud alcoholics, and slightly just a collective of nice assholes, but I'll be damned if it's not the perfect place in the world for someone like me. Don't get me wrong, there are times that I like being able to walk somewhere and not run into someone I know, but truly that's the thing I miss the most. How close knit we truly are when we get to the bare bones of it. The music scene, the beer, the food, then you and me. I even find myself missing those feet of snow that nearly kill us every winter, just something about being around my people. My family. In the famous words of a very close friend of mine, "I'm just a kid from Grand Rapids". And that's something that makes me happy.

- M.H.

www.ingramcontent.com/pod-product-compliance
Lightning Source LLC
Chambersburg PA
CBHW020556220526
45463CB00006B/2326